WOMEN IN TODAY'S WORLD

VOLUME 2, ISSUE 1 OF BRILLOPEDIA

SUBHA LAKSHMI K

I dedicate this book to respected madam Smt.P.Geetha Jeevan Minister for Social Welfare and Women Empowerment of Tamil Nadu.

Contents

Preface

"Start writing, no matter what. The water does not flow until the faucet is turned on".

-Louis L'Amour

Hundreds of students and professors are contributing their work to Brain Booster Articles, we are here to provide ample information about Law and Contemporary issues. Our aim is to provide a platform for today's generation to express their views and ideas on law and contemporary law.

Publication

This research paper is published in volume 2, issue 1 of Brillopedia

Author

Subha Lakshmi K

CHAPTER ONE

ABSTRACT

Women is said to be the aspect of power. It believed that women are created to fulfill almighty needs of the world. On this Women's Day we are discussing all about women and her dignity and problems faced by her. A woman is known for the nature of love and also the burden bearer of the family. This article speaks about women and her power and how she is in the world today. And also mainly speaks about the troubles and difficulties faced by a woman and how she is affected. If hundred women starts her travel in the path to progress of life the first 90% of them stays back due to ignorance and negativity. The other 10% only starts their progress of life with lots of struggles and they become the real achievers and winners. This article explains women empowerment gender discrimination, participation of women in politics, work, cultures and sciences, journalism, her participation in entertainment, sports, culinary arts etc. The main aim this article is to show the status of women in the past, present and future. A woman shines as a caretaker, an educator, a conscience farmer and also an entrepreneur. She proves herself that she is stronger than men. And let discuss about the issues faced by women and what are the measures taken to ensure the welfare of women in legal aspect.

KEYWORDS: empowerment, politics, journalism, caretaker, educator, entrepreneur.

CHAPTER TWO

INTRODUCTON

We are living in the generation where we should be proud for being a woman. Nowadays in every field women are proving that she is mentally stronger than the men who are physically strong. Women are irremovable from everybody's life taking the role as a mother, a wife, a sister and a daughter. That is why it said that, "behind every successful man there is a woman". There are still women who facing lots of failure and still keeps shining. During French Revolution itself men and women are started treating equally and started entering into politics. During the revolution eight hours work, wages for their work, right for voting was given them. During the early 19th century many conflict started creating awareness amongst the women in the world countries. Then they started realizing their strength. Many struggle moments was started to abolish cruelty against women, disgracing women, dominating them for being a woman during those periods. Solution of these struggles there raised the World Women's Day in the year 1913, on the 8th day of March.

CHAPTER THREE

WOMEN AND HER RIGHTS

Women rights imply rights of women all over the world and also girl children. In the 19th century it was started from women rights and later in the 20th and 21st century it was the base of the concept of feminism. In some countries these rights act are institutionalized are supported with their local custom and behavior. But in the other countries rights for women are ignored and are totally suppressed. During 16th and 17th century lots of witch experiment was made and throughout Europe lots of people were hanged, from those 75%-95% was women. Major rights which were given to women in some countries are:

- Equal work
- Right to vote
- Property Rights

<u>WOMEN AND HER LEGAL RIGHTS</u>

In most of the developing countries there is lack of lack of legal knowledge was a major obstacle for growth of women's situation. International organizations like United Nations council not only consists passing the laws but also says these laws gets justice and made feel the practice of law. Also lets them the knowledge of law. Therefore, it is the duty of the states to popularize these types of laws without ignorance. Further, these laws should be clearly explained to the people. In 1993 United Nations tried to stop violence against women.

CHAPTER FOUR

GENDER DISCRIMINATION

Many women freedom movements focus to bring an end for the discrimination against women. There are lots of definitions against gender discrimination. According to the European Court of Human Rights, the freedom of discrimination also includes not only the states obligation to treat women in the same way but also the obligations to treat in different way to the women who are in different situations. Therefore not only equality is importance there must be equity everywhere. Sometimes states must differentiate women in certain situation and give more importance than women in situations like maternity, sexual harassment etc. Violence against women is also a form of women discrimination. In detail there must be gender equality where men and women should be treated equally. So, there must not be any discrimination based on gender. And in the social context there must be democracy where men and women should be treated equally without any situations from equal pay for equal work in every other field to achieve gender equality.

CHAPTER FIVE

WOMEN EMPOWERMENT

Women Empowerment means the process of upgrading women. Empowerment can be defined in many ways. However when we speak about women empowerment also includes accepting and allowing women who are out of decision making. Empowerment means the process of empowering their personal own life and social life. If they get an opportunity to access without any limitations and restrictions in education, work they are empowered. Women empowerment is to determining the problems in the society and to equipping and allowing to take decisions. Women empowerment has changed into biggest discussions among growth and economy. Empowering women can help the nation to grow faster.

CHAPTER SIX

WOMEN IN THE PAST, PRESENT AND FUTURE

- **Women In Previous Times :**

In the previous times women are only allowed to participate only in the fields allocated for women. During the period of 1975-85 women were living in the small circle like separate bus, college for only girls. Before some years there was lots of men domination in the society where women was mostly dominated and ignored. In every place the voice of women was very low and does not even have any rights to make own decisions. Women were under the ownership of men. Women were considered only to be inside the four walls. Most of the women were affected by poor health and malnutrition. Earlier, women were mostly uneducated, some were educated but that was not enough for the improvement of women. Maternal grandmothers had a practice of eating whatever is leftover at home. These were the myths followed by the people in those days. After only participating these myths the mindset every women was put down like the thought that they does not have the capability of questioning and are not able to be practical. Therefore, they follow these myths blindly and some are still in a down situation. Women status in the western countries has gone through some substantial changes.

- **Women In The Current Situation:**

These days' women began to be remarkable and well known in the profession and also in the society. Nowadays, women share the equal position with men. In some places there is participation of women in every field. United Nations study shows that two-thirds of the illiterates are women. Now the society started treating women in a special place. The great law-giver says that, if the women are honored then there lies the god. In Hinduism there is no man are allowed to attend any rituals without his wife. There are big list of women achievers in India. The society looks differently today. If women want to achieve she breaks every obstacle including family. The United Nations flagship analyses the issues of women from family, employment, and cruelty against her. Status of women to has widely changed from housewives to CEOs. They are establishing themselves in every field socially, politically and economically. Many have started setting milestone in every field. Some of the achievements of women are given below.

- **Women Towards The Future:**

The status of women is increasingly outstanding nowadays. In future if there is a complete removal of social evils like cruelty of women, inequality, dowry and female foeticide. Special laws to safeguard women and girl children should be developed. Everyone should understand the importance of strong women and independent female. A future woman has the capability of full of success in e very field they pursue. Today's women have started breaking the foolish restrains and hindrance of the path to success. They are emerging as physically, mentally, and economically stronger day-by-day. This is just a begging of their successful journey and this journey continues in the future.

CHAPTER SEVEN

ACHIEVEMENTS OF WOMEN IN INDIA

- **Justice M.FathimaBeevi**was the first female judge who was appointed to the Supreme Court of India in the year 1989.
- In the year 1887 **AnandibhaiGopalrao** Joshi became the first Indian female physician and also she was the first Indian woman who was trained for Western medicine and she also the first woman to travel to the United States of America.
- In the year 1979, the first woman to win in the Nobel Peace Prize was **Mother Terasa**. She was the first woman to give her whole life to social work.
- **Indira Gandhi** was the first woman Prime Minister of India from the year 1966 to 1997. She was named as the "Woman of the Millennium" in a poll that was organized by BBC in 1999. She first woman to receive the Bharat Ratna award.
- In the year 1972, **KiranBedi** became the first woman officer in India for joining the Indian Police Service. Moreover she was the woman who was appointed as the United Nations Civil Police adviser.
- **PrathibhaPatil**was the first woman President of India from July 2007 to July 2012.
- The only womenboxer who medal in every six World Championships is**MangteChungneijang Mary Kom**is also known as Mary Kom. She was the only Indian women boxer to win a gold medal in Asian Games in the year 2014.
- Kalpanachawla was the first Indian women to reach the space in the year 1997 as mission specialist and a primary robotic arm operator.

Every woman achieves their goals by breaking all the obstacles.

CHAPTER EIGHT

PARTICIPATION OF WOMEN IN POLITICS

Political participation of women not only denotes the right of voting it also relates participation in decision making process, political activism, political consciousness, etc. In India participation of women in political parties and public offices is at a very lower stage. But women's participation in political activism and voting are the strongest of all. Participation of women in the political party has increased the demand for political rights. All the political part starting joining women has started competing. Many women's organization emerged in the early 1900s. Bharat SreeMahamandal was one of the earliest women's organization formed in the year 1910 which focused on helping women. The only solution for women to shine in politics is women empowerment. In the year 2009 June, the Indian National Congress nominated a women who became the first speak of LokSabha. Many women politicians have set a milestone in the field of politics. Indira Gandhi was the first Prime Minister of Indian. NirmalaSitharaman was the India's first full-time finance minister.Many challenges like sexual harassment, gender discrimination, illiteracy, are faced by women to taking part in the politics. In the year 2019 there were only 10 women Head of the State and only 13 women Head of the Government across 22 countries. But today 1 in 4 parliamentary seats are held by women.

CHAPTER NINE

PARTICIPATION OF WOMEN IN WORK

In today's strongest business world, companies mostly face the problem of gender imbalance. If there is no issues in gender balance right then they should have the responsibility of retaining. According to research world wide the leadership positions of women are very less. Only 4.9% of women take place in the leadership position out of 500 fortune companies. India is one of the countries to given the lowest number of women labour for as percentage of 22. Recent days most of the companies are seeing the value of women and they believe that every woman has the capability of ensuring the progress of the company. Many more companies recognize that a woman brings crucial innovations to the field and it helps to achieve everything. It is believed that women have the power of decision-making, and have the capability of deciding the career choices and building ownership.

CHAPTER TEN

PARTICIPATION OF WOMEN IN CULTURES, SPORTS AND ENTERTAINMENT

Women are said to be the guardians for the culture of the society. It is believe that the culture is protected by women.India is the country where cultures and customs are followed continuously. Even in the Indian families traditionally are followed in hierarchical manner. Right from marriages the tradition is followed. Mostly in India only monogamous marriages are allowed. Rangoli is also a traditional practice of Indian women. In the 1991, the High Court of Kerala restricted allowing women above the age of 10 and below the age of 50 was not allowed inside the temple in Sabarimala Shrine. But the Supreme Court of Indian on 28 September 2018 said that discriminating women on every ground even in religion is against the constitution.

In the present, participation of women in sports is growing rapidly. School is the place where the passion for sports is born.Fourteen percent of women in China between the ages 19 and 29 did not participate in the sports activities in school. Even in Japan 84% stood away from sports. The research from woman and Sport reports that 76% chances of women are interested in sports starts from sporting activities at school. In the years 1970s and 1980s was a turning point of the sports field was the participation of women in sports activities has been increased. Now the trend continues in the sports field.According to the statistics only 22 women out of 997 athletes competed in the modern Olympics in the year 1990.

Participation of women in field of entertainment in every roles including a film directors, actresses, cinematographers, film producers, film critics etc with lots of hindrances. The US film industry gave more importance to women in participation of English language and also started many academies, while others countries has the discrimination of women even in this field. Woman was always great in this field but simultaneously they were less paid. In recent times, women are contributing to this field and are reaching their heights.Analysis says that across 11 countries world 31 percent of speaking characters were women and only 23 percent of women are protagonist and 21 percent of women are film makers. There is a lot of expectations for women film from on -creen and also in off-screen.

CHAPTER ELEVEN

ISSUES FACED BY WOMEN TODAY

There are numerous problems and issues are faced by women in their day to day life. Some of the problems are given below:

- Child Marriage in age which they wanted to study.
- Job opportunity equal to men but very less pay. It can be seemed that women employment has grown but in some points they get only small amount of pay for their work.
- Most of the women are ignored for leadership responsibilities.
- Violence and cruelty against women. Sexual Harassment is the major issue of women which are not still rectified.
- In most of the places women are still judgmental and criticized.
- Defining a woman only because she is beautiful from outside.
- Marriage before her financial independence is a big drawback for today's women.
- A man can continue his education without any restriction. But women havelimitations even in studies.
- Cruelly treated in workplace and home by some heartless women itself.
- Decreased wages even the work is more than men.
- Sexual harassment for women in the field of film and entertainment industries.
- Rape is the biggest major issue in current situation.
- Sex torture after marriage is known as marital rape.
- Acid attack if the girl refuses a love.
- Morphing photos and uploading in internet for refusing and rejections.
- Criticism for wearing any kind of dresses.

- Times are passing into new generation but there is still the practice of dowry.
- The begging point of issues against women starts from female foeticide and killing of girl children.
- Ignoring women during their menstrual period.

CHAPTER TWELVE

Law

CONSTITUTIONAL PROVISIONS AND PREVILEGES

- Article 14 gives the right of equality before law for women.
- Article 42 says that the state shall make provision related to work and maternity relief.
- Article 47 says that the state shall raise the level of nutrition and standard of living for people.

LAWS RELATING TO WOMEN

- Commission of Sati (Prevention) Act, 1987.
- Criminal Law (Amendment) Act, 1983.
- Dowry Prohibition Act, 1961.
- Immoral Traffic (Prevention) Act, 1956.
- Indecent Representation of Women (Prohibition) Act, 1986.
- National Commission for Women Act, 1990.
- Prohibition of Sexual Harassment of Women at Workplace Bill, 2010.
- Protection of Women from Domestic Violence Act, 2005.

LAWS RELATING TO WORKING WOMEN

- Contract Labour (Regulation and Abolition) Act, 1976.
- Employees State Insurance Act, 1948.
- Equal Remuneration Act, 1976.
- Factories (Amendment) Act, 1948.
- Maternity Benefit Act, 1961 (Amended in 1995).
- Plantation Labour act, 1951.

OFFENCES AGAINST WOMEN AND CHILDREN UNDER THE INDIAN PENAL CODE

The Indian Penal Code, 1860 has given some of the provisions to penalize the victim for the offences against women. Some of the specific sections are given below under IPC:

- Section 326A and section 326B lays down acid attack and the punishment for acid attacks.
- Section 375, 376A, 376B, 376B, 376C, 376E explains about rape and punishments for rape.
- Section 376 and 511 for attempt to commit rape.
- Section 302, 304B, and 306 for Murder, Dowry death, Abetment of Suicide etc.
- Section 354A for Sexual harassment.
- Section 354C for Voyeurism.
- Section 345D for Stalking.

CHAPTER THIRTEEN

ROLE OF WOMEN AS A CARETAKER, CONSCIENCE FARMERS AND EDUCATORS

Right from rural to urban women plays an extraordinary role in caring the faming. That is why it is said that there is woman behind every successful man. Some of the international study shows that women help the families to accept the change from new realities and challenges.

Women have contributed a lot for transferring the society from literates to illiterates. Many researchessay that educating women is the key to improve the agricultural productivity and to enhance the status of girl children and women. In a family it is the mother who stimulates and boost up their children who might be in both gender to attend and stay in school. It is to be noted that survival of the future is in the hands of women.

CHAPTER FOURTEEN

CONCLUSION

We are in the world were women should be appreciated for her each and every achievements. Women are known as the multitaskers. They are mentally and physically brave. There are now many organizations have started in India to close the mouth who said, opportunities for are women still ignored. Every boy children must be taught to respect women from their small age. There is no future without women. The strength and energy of women still pushes the world forward. Women are the backbone of the development of economics and civilizations. Mahabaratham says that, every woman is considered to goddess MaryMatha and Durga Devi. A man one who does not respect woman he is merely considered as the worst character. If the issues of women want to be control there should be equality all over the world. Finally I conclude that from this Women's Day we shall respect every woman and support her and take every effort to create a protected environment.

www.ingramcontent.com/pod-product-compliance
Lightning Source LLC
Chambersburg PA
CBHW072145150726
48002CB00004B/1640